COUNTY DURHAM

Wit & Humour

STANLEY CUTHBERT

BRADWELL
BOOKS

Published by Bradwell Books
9 Orgreave Close Sheffield S13 9NP
Email: books@bradwellbooks.co.uk
Compiled by Stanley Cuthbert

British Library Cataloguing in Publication Data: a catalogue record for this book is
available from the British Library.

1st Edition
ISBN: 9781910551226

Print: Gomer Press, Llandysul, Ceredigion SA44 4JL
Design by: Jenks Design
Illustrations: ©Tim O'Brien 2015

Two elderly ladies in Castle Eden had been friends for many decades. Over the years, they had shared all kinds of fun but of late their activities had been limited to meeting a few times a week to play cards. One day, they were playing pontoon when one looked at the other and said, "Now don't get crusty with us, pet. Ah know we've been friends for a long time but Ah just canna think of yewer name. Ah've thought and thought, but Ah canna remember it. Please tell us what yewer name is." Her friend got cross and, for at least three minutes, she just stared and glared at her. Finally she said, "How soon do yer need te know?"

A teacher at a school in Stockton-on-Tees was having a little trouble getting her Year 11 pupils to understand grammar. "These are what we call the pronouns," she said, "We use them with verbs like this: I am, you are, he/she is." The pupils looked at her with glazed expressions.

Trying a different tack, she said, "Lauren, give me a sentence with the pronoun, 'I' in it."

Lauren began, "I is…"

"No, no, no, no, no NO, NO!" shouted the teacher, "Never, 'I is', always, 'I am'… now try again."

Lauren looked puzzled and a little hurt, thought a while then began again more quietly, "I... am...the ninth letter of the alphabet."

The magistrate at Durham County Court spoke sharply to the defendant, "But if you saw the lady driving towards you, why didn't you give her half the road?"

"Ah were going to, yer Honour," replied the motorist, "…as soon as Ah could work out which half she wanted."

Two rival cricketers from Burnmoor and Esh Winning were having a chat.

"The local team wants me to play for them very badly," said the man from Burnmoor."

"Well," said his friend, "You're just the man for the job."

A lad from Chester-le-Street went into a French restaurant in Durham and asked the waiter, "Have you got frog's legs?"
He said, "Yes," so the lad said, "Well hop into the kitchen and get us a chip butty."

A poor bloke from Escomb nearly drowned in a bowl of muesli – he was pulled in by a strong currant.

Simon was down on his luck so he thought he would try getting a few odd jobs by calling at the posh houses in Wynyard. After a few "no ways", a guy in one of the big houses thought he would give him a break and says, "The porch needs painting so I'll give you £50 to paint it for me."

"You're a life-saver, mister," says Simon, "Arl dee it reet away!" Time passes until…

"There yer go, Ah'm all done with the painting."

"Well, here's your £50," says the homeowner, handing over some crisp tenners.

"Thanks very much," says Simon, pocketing the money, "Oh and by the way, it's a Ferrari, not a Porsche!"

Just before the big race at Sedgefield, the trainer was giving last minute instructions to the jockey and appeared to slip something into the horse's mouth just as a steward walked by.

"What was that?" inquired the steward.

"Oh nowt," said the trainer, "just a polo."

He offered one to the steward and had one himself. After the suspicious steward had left the scene, the trainer continued with his instructions.

"Just keep on the rail. You're on a dead cert. The only thing that could possibly pass you down the home straight is either the steward or me."

A Citizens fan was watching Durham City A. F. C. thrash the Bedlington Terriers in the Northern League.

In the packed New Ferens Park stadium, there was only one empty seat – right next to him.

"Who does that seat belong to?" asked Dave from the row behind.

"Ah got the ticket for ma missus," replied the Citizens fan.

"But why isn't she here?"

"Ah'm afraid she died in a tragic accident."

"So you're keeping the seat vacant as a mark of respect," said Dave.

"No," said the Citizens fan, "Ah offered it to all of ma friends."

"Then why didn't they take it?" asked a puzzled Dave.

"They've all gone to the funeral."

A lad from Stanley was bragging to his mate: "Ma computer beat us at chess, but it were no match for us at kick boxing."

An elderly couple from Barnard Castle are sitting at the dining table in their semi-detached house talking about making preparations for writing their wills. Bill says to his missus, Edna, "Ah've been thinking, hinny, if Ah go first to meet ma maker Ah dinna want yer to be on yewer own for too long. In fact, Ah think yer could do worse than marry Colin in the Chemists or Dave with the fruit stall in the market. They'd provide for yer and look after yer when Ah'm gone."

"That's very kind of yer to think about us like that, Bill," replied Edna, "But Ah've already made ma own arrangements!"

Derek and Duncan were long-time neighbours in Bishop Auckland. Every time, Derek saw Duncan coming round to his house, his heart sank. This was because he knew that, as always, Duncan would be visiting him in order to borrow something and he was fed up with it.

"I'm not going to let Duncan get away with it this time," he said quietly to his wife, "Watch what I'm about to do."

"Hi there, I wondered if you were thinking about using your hedge trimmer this afternoon?" asked Duncan.

"Oh, I'm very sorry," said Derek, trying to look apologetic, "but I'm actually going to be using it all afternoon."

"In that case," replied Duncan with a big grin, "You won't be using your golf clubs, will you? Mind if I borrow them?"

A lawyer from Berwick-upon-Tweed and a businessman from Durham ended up sitting next to each other on a long-haul flight.

The lawyer started thinking that he could have some fun at the man from Durham's expense and asked him if he'd like to play a fun game. The businessman was tired and just wanted to relax. He politely declined the offer and tried to sleep. The lawyer persisted, explaining, "I ask you a question, and if you don't know the answer, you pay me just £5; you ask me one, and if I don't know the answer, I will pay you £500."

This got the businessman a little more interested and he finally agreed to play the game.

The lawyer asked the first question, "What's the distance from the Earth to the moon?"

The man from Durham said nothing, but reached into his pocket, pulled out a five-pound note and handed it to the lawyer.

Now, it was his turn to ask a question. He asked the lawyer, "What goes up a hill with three legs, and comes down with four?"

The lawyer scratched his head. He looked the question up on his laptop and searched the web. He sent emails to his most well-read friends. He used the air-phone to call his colleagues in Berwick-upon-Tweed, but he still came up with nothing.

After over an hour of searching, he finally gave up. He woke up the businessman and handed him £500. The man pocketed the cash smugly and dozed off again.

The lawyer was wild with curiosity and wanted to know the answer. He shook the businessman awake. "Well? What goes up a hill with three legs and comes down with four?" he demanded.

The businessman reached into his pocket, handed the lawyer £5 and went straight back to sleep.

Man: "I'm off to see a show some ex-miners are putting on in their local theatre in County Durham."

Mate: "Consett?"

Man: "No, more of a variety show really."

How do you get a sweet old County Durham granny to swear? Get another sweet old County Durham granny to shout "BINGO!"

Q: What did one ocean say to the other ocean?

A: Nothing, they just waved.

Two elderly ladies were enjoying a bottle of brown in their local in Staindrop.

One said to the other, "Was it love at first sight when yer met yewer late husband?"

"No, Ah dinna think so," came the reply, "Ah didn't know how much money he had when Ah first met him!"

Fred's wife has been missing for over a week. The police liaison officer warned him to prepare for the worst…so Fred went to the charity shop to get all her clothes back.

A man from Stanley said to his wife, "Get yewer coat on, hinny. Ah's gan doon te club."

His wife said, "That's nice. Yer 'ave nae taken us oot for years". He said, "Yewer nae coming with us...Ah's turning heating off when Ah go oot".

A police officer was patrolling the lanes outside Castle Barnard one night, when he noticed a car swerving all over the road. Quickly, he turned on his lights and siren and pulled the driver over. "Sir, do you know you're all over the road? Please step out of the car."

When the man got out of the car, the policeman told him to walk in a straight line.

"Ah'd be happy te, offisher," said the drunk, "If yer can just get the line te stop moving aboot."

Q: What's the difference between a new husband and a new dog?

A: After a year, the dog is still excited to see you.

A bloke from Bishop Auckland goes into an artist's studio and asks if the artist could paint a picture of him surrounded by beautiful, scantily clad women. The artist agrees but he is intrigued by this strange request. He asks his new client why he wants such a picture painted and the bloke says, "Well, if Ah die before ma missus when she finds this painting she'll wonder which one Ah spent all ma money on!"

The next day the bloke's wife goes into the artist's studio and asks him to paint her wearing a big diamond necklace and matching earrings.

"Of course, madam," says the artist, "but may I ask why?"

"Well," replies the woman, "if Ah die before ma husband Ah want his new woman to be frantic searching for all ma jewellery!"

A County Durham man is driving through Northumberland when he passes a farmer standing in the middle of a huge field. He pulls the car over and watches the farmer standing stock-still, doing absolutely nothing. Intrigued, the man walks over to the farmer and asks him, "Excuse me sir, but what are you doing?"

The farmer replies, "I'm trying to win a Nobel Prize."

"How?" Asks the puzzled County Durham man.

"Well," says the farmer, "I heard they give the prize to people who are outstanding in their field."

A well-known academic from the University of Cumbria was giving a lecture on the philosophy of language at Durham University. He came to a curious aspect of English grammar.

"You will note," said the somewhat stuffy scholar, "That in the English language, two negatives can mean a positive, but it is never the case that two positives can mean a negative."

To which someone at the back responded, "Yeah, yeah."

At a cricket match in Willington, a fast bowler sent one down and it just clipped the bail. As nobody yelled "Ow's att," the batsman picked up the bail and replaced it. He looked at the umpire and said, "Windy today, ain't it?"

"Aye," said the umpire, "Mind it dinnit blow your cap off when you're walking back to the pavilion."

In Newton Aycliffe, two neighbours greet each other over the garden fence.

"Hello, bonny-lad? What's astir?"

"Poor old granda's fell down deed this morning," says the neighbour, "He was out in the garden pulling up cabbages and he went, just like that – we think it was his heart."

"What a shame," commiserates the man next door, "What're you ganna do now?"

"Open a tin of peas," says the neighbour.

A policeman stops a drunk wandering the streets of Stanley at four in the morning and says, "Can you explain why you are out at this hour, sir?"

The drunk replies, "If A were able to explain meself, A would 'ave been home with the missus ages ago."

Police arrested two kids in Consett the other day; one was drinking battery acid, the other was eating fireworks. They charged one and let the other one off.

A DEFRA Inspector goes to a small farm near Middleton-in-Teesdale and knocks the door of the humble, tied cottage. A young boy opens the door and asks what business the man has on his parent's property.

"I've come to inspect the farm for compliance with EU regulations, my boy. Where's your father?"

"Yer canna speak to him, he's busy," says the surly child.

"I shall speak to him. He's had notice of my visit," the Inspector retorted firmly.

"Well, he's feeding the pigs at the moment," says the boy, "But you'll be able te tell me Da easy enough – he's the one wearing a hat!"

One freezing cold December day, two blondes went for a walk in Hamsterley Forest in search of the perfect Christmas tree. Finally, after five hours looking, one turns to the other and says crossly, "That's it, I've had enough. I'm chopping down the next fir tree we see, whether it's decorated or not!"

A reporter from The Durham Times was covering the Wearside League and went to see Horden Colliery Welfare A.F.C. versus Spennymoor Town Reserves. One of the Colliers players looked so old, he went over to him and said, "You know you might be the oldest man playing in the league. How do you do it at your age?"

The man replied, "Ah drink six pints o' broon iv'ry night, smoke two packets of tabs a day, and eat loads of bacon butties."

"Wow, that is incredible!" said the reporter, "How old did you say you were?"

"Twenty-two," said the player proudly.

An Easington couple, Enid and Sidney, are having matrimonial difficulties and seek the advice of a counsellor. The couple are shown into a room where the counsellor asks Enid what problems, in her opinion, she faces in her relationship with Sidney.

"Well," she starts, "he shows me no affection, I don't seem to be important to him anymore. We don't share the same interests and I don't think he loves me at all." Enid has tears in her eyes as the counsellor walks over to her, gives her a big hug and kisses her firmly on the lips.

Sidney looks on in passive disbelief. The counsellor turns to Sidney and says, "This is what Enid needs once a day for the next month. Can you see that she gets it?"

Sidney looks unsettled, "Well, Ah can drop her off iv'ry day other than Wednesdays when Ah play snooker and Sundays when Ah go fishing!"

A man went to the doctor and said, "Ah've just been playing rugby for Horden Welfare and Ah felt fine but Ah got back home and Ah found that when Ah touched ma legs, ma arms, ma head, ma belly and everywhere else, it really hurt."

After a careful examination the doctor said, "You've broken your finger."

Two hawks were sitting on their perch at Walworth Castle Bird of Prey Centre.

"Look at that speed!" one hawk said to the other as a jet fighter plane roared over their heads on its way to RAF Spadeadam in Cumbria.

"Hmph!" snorted the second hawk. "You would fly fast too if your tail was on fire!"

A policeman stops a man in a car in the middle of Darlington with a sheep in the front seat.

"Alright, what are you doing with that sheep?" He asks. "You should take it to a zoo."

The following week, the same policeman sees the same man again with the sheep in the front seat of the car. Both of them are wearing sunglasses. The policeman pulls him over. "I thought you were going to take that sheep to the zoo?"

The man replies, "I did. We had such a good time we are going to the coast this weekend!"

One night an old couple in Peterlee were lying in bed. The husband was falling asleep but the wife was in a romantic mood and wanted to talk.

She said, "Yer used to hold ma hand when we were courting, man."

Wearily he reached across, held her hand for a second and tried to get back to sleep.

A few moments later she said, "Then yer used to kiss us, man."

Mildly irritated, he reached across, gave her a peck on the cheek and settled down to sleep.

Thirty seconds later she said, "Then yer used to nibble ma neck, man."

Angrily, he threw back the bedclothes and got out of bed.

"Where are yer going?" she asked.

"Te get ma teeth!"

Man: "My uncle's from County Durham."
His mate: "Crook?"
Man: "Do you mind! He's a law-abiding citizen!"38

A police officer arrived at the scene of a major pile up on the A167.

The officer runs over to the front car and asks the driver, "Are you seriously hurt?"

The driver turns to the officer and says, "How the heck should I know? Do I look like a lawyer?"

Four fonts walk into a bar. The barman says, "Oi – get out! We don't want your type in here"

A bloke walked up to the foreman of a road laying gang in Spennymoor and asked for a job. "Ah got nowt for yer today," said the foreman, looking up from his newspaper. "But if yer walk half a mile down there, yer'll find the gang and yer can see if yer like the work. Ah can put yer on te list for tomorrow." "That's great, boss," said the bloke as he wandered off down the road.

At the end of the shift, the man walked past the foreman and shouted, "Thanks, boss. See you in the morning."

The foreman looked up from his paper and called back, "You've enjoyed yersel then?"

"Yeah, Ah 'ave!" the bloke shouted, "But can Ah 'ave a shovel or a pick te lean on like the rest of the gang tomorrow?"

Sam worked in a telephone marketing company in Durham. One day he walked into his boss's office and said, "I'll be honest with you, I know the economy isn't great, but I have three companies after me, and, with respect, I would like to ask for a pay rise."

After a few minutes of haggling, his manager finally agreed to a 5% pay rise, and Sam happily got up to leave.

"By the way," asked the boss as Sam went to the door, "Which three companies are after you?"

"The electric company, the water company, and the phone company," Sam replied.

A farmer was driving along a country road near the village of Edmundbyers with a large load of fertiliser. A little boy, playing in front of his cottage, saw him and called out, "What do yer 'ave on yewer truck?"

"Fertiliser," the farmer replied.

"What are yer ganna do with it?" asked the little boy.

"Put it on strawberries," answered the farmer.

"Yer ought to live here," the little boy advised him. "We put sugar and cream on ours."

It was a quiet night in Tanfield and a man and his wife were fast asleep, when there was an unexpected knock on the door. The man looked at his alarm clock. It was half past three in the morning. "I'm not getting out of bed at this time," he thought and rolled over.

There was another louder knock.

"Aren't you going to answer that?" asked his wife irritably.

So the man dragged himself out of bed and went downstairs. He opened the door to find a strange man standing outside. It didn't take the homeowner long to realise the man was absolutely lashed.

"Hi there, bonny-lad," slurred the stranger. "Can yer give us a push?"

"No, I'm sorry I most certainly can't. It's half past three in the morning and I was in bed," said the man and he slammed the front door.

He went back up to bed and told his wife what happened. "That wasn't very nice of you," she said. "Remember that night we broke down in the pouring rain on the way to pick the kids up from the babysitter, and you had to knock on that man's door to get us started again? What would have happened if he'd told us to get lost?"

"But the man who just knocked on our door was drunk," replied her husband.

"Well, we can at least help move his car somewhere safe and sort him out a taxi," said his wife. "He needs our help."

So the husband got out of bed again, got dressed, and went downstairs. He opened the door, but couldn't to see the stranger anywhere so he shouted, "Hey, do you still want a push?"

In answer, he heard a voice call out, "Yes, please, man!"

So, still unable to see the stranger, he shouted, "Where are you?"

"Ah's over here, bonny-lad," the stranger replied, "on yewer swing."

Phil's nephew came to him with a problem. "I have my choice of two women," he said, with a worried frown, "A beautiful, penniless young girl whom I love dearly, and a rich widow who I don't really love."

"Follow your heart," Phil counselled, "marry the lass you love."

"Very well, Uncle Phil," said the nephew, "That's sound advice. Thank you."

"You're welcome," replied Phil with a smile, "By the way, where does the widow live?"

An ex-miner was collecting for charity around Dean bank. He rang a doorbell and an old woman answered the door.

"Would yer like to make a contribution to the Ferryhill Town brass band benevolent fund, hinny?" he asked.

The old woman put her hand to her ear and said, "Eh?"

He repeated his patter several times, getting louder each time but the old woman's reaction remained the same.

In the end he stomped off down the garden path and was halfway across the road, when the old woman shouted, "And close me blooming gate, man."

"Stuff yer gate," he muttered under his breath.

"And stuff the Ferryhill brass band benevolent fund," shouted the old woman.

Three old boys, all a bit hard of hearing, were playing golf one fine day at the Ramside Hall Hotel Golf Club.

One remarked to the other, "Windy, ain't it?"

"No," the second man replied, "It's Thursday..."

"So am I," chimed in the third man, "Let's have a beer."

At a school in Easington, the maths teacher poses a question to little Lee, "If I give £500 to your dad on 12% interest per annum, what will I get back after two years."

"Nowt," says Lee.

"I am afraid you know nothing about maths, Lee," says the teacher crossly.

"Ah's afraid too, sir," replies Lee, "Yer dinnit knaa nowt about ma Da."

Did you hear about the dyslexic man who walked into a bra?

A passenger in a taxi tapped the driver on the shoulder to ask him something.

The driver screamed, lost control of the cab, nearly hit a bus, drove up over the curb and stopped just inches from a large plate glass window.

For a few moments everything was silent in the cab, then the driver said, "Please, don't ever do that again. You scared the daylights out of me."

The passenger, who was also frightened, apologised and said he didn't realise that a tap on the shoulder could frighten him so much, to which the driver replied, "I'm sorry, it's really not your fault at all. Today is my first day driving a cab. I've been driving a hearse for the last twenty-five years."

A high-rise building was going up in Durham and three steel erectors sat on a girder having their lunch.

"Oh, no, not cheese and pickle again," said Jim, the first one, "If I get the same again tomorrow, I'll jump off the girder.'

Harry opened his packet. "Oh, no, not a chicken salad with mayo and lettuce on granary," he said. "If I get the same again tomorrow, I'll jump off too."

Owen, the third man, opened his lunch. "Oh, no, not another potato sandwich," he said. "If I get the same again tomorrow, I'll follow you two off the girder."

The next day, Jim got cheese and pickle. Without delay, he jumped. Harry saw he had chicken salad with mayo and lettuce on granary, and with a wild cry, he leapt too. Then the third man, Owen, opened his lunchbox. "Oh, no," he said. "Potato sandwiches." And he too jumped.

The foreman, who had overheard their conversation, reported what had happened, and the funerals were held together.

"If only I'd known," sobbed Jim's wife.

"If only he'd said," wailed Harry's wife.

"I don't understand it at all," said Owen's wife. "He always made his own sandwiches."

A farmer from Cheviot Hills in Northumberland once visited a farmer based near Lanchester. The visitor asked, "How big is yewer farm?" to which the County Durham farmer replied, "Can yer see those trees over there? That's the boundary of ma farmland".

"Is that all?" said the Northumberland farmer, "It takes us three days to drive to the boundary of ma farm."

The Lanchester man looked at him and said, "Ah had a car like that once."

The nervous young batsman playing for the Annfield Plain C.C. was having a very bad day. In a quiet moment in the game, he muttered to the one of his team mates, "Well, I suppose you've seen worse players."

There was no response...so he said it again, "I said 'I guess you've seen worse players'."

His team mate looked at him and answered, "I heard you the first time. I was just trying to think..."

At a pub in Chester-le-street a newcomer asked a local man, "Have you lived here all your life?"

The old man took a sip of his ale and, after a long pause, replied, "A dinna knaa yet!"

An Englishman, an Irishman, a Scotsman, a Norwegian, a Dutchman, a Dane, an Italian, a Hungarian, a Nigerian, a Russian, an Indian, an Australian, an American, and a Filipino walk into a club in Hartlepool. The doorman says, "Sorry, lads, but Ah canna let youse-lot in without a Thai."

A plain Jane from Cornforth goes to see Madame Grizelda, a fortune-teller, and asks about her future love life.

Madame Grizelda tells her, "Two men are madly in love with you – Mark and Maurice."

"Who will be the lucky one?" asks Jane excitedly.

Madame Grizelda answers, "Maurice will marry you, and Mark will be the lucky one."

Did you hear about the fight in the chip shop last week? Six fish got battered!

Many years ago, a miner fell down pit-shaft at Astley Green Colliery.

The deputy shouted, "Have yer broken owt, lad?"

"Nae," called back the miner, "There's nowt much to break down here!"

There were two fish in a tank, one says, "You man the guns, I'll drive."

A man rushed into Darlington Memorial and asked a nurse for a cure for hiccups. Grabbing a cup of water, the nurse quickly splashed it into the man's face.

"What did yer do that for?" screamed the man, wiping his face. "Well, you don't have the hiccups now, do you?" said the nurse. "No," replied the man. "But owwer lass out in the car does."

Did you hear about the last wish of the henpecked husband of a house-proud wife?

He asked to have his ashes scattered on the carpet.

A Stanhope woman called Sue was still not married at thirty-five and she was getting really tired of going to family weddings especially because her old Aunt Maud always came over and said, "You're next!"

It made Sue so annoyed, she racked her brains to figure out how to get Aunt Maud to stop. Sadly, an old uncle died and there was a big family funeral. Sue spotted Aunt Maud in the crematorium, walked over, pointed at the coffin and said, with a big smile, "You're next!"

One day at Shotley Bridge Hospital in Consett, a group of primary school children were being given a tour. A nurse showed them the x-ray machines and asked them if they had ever had broke a bone.

One little boy raised his hand, "I did!"

"Did it hurt?" the nurse asked.

"No!" he replied.

"Wow, you must be a very brave boy!" said the nurse. "What did you break?"

"Ma sister's arm!"

A man and his wife were walking past the swanky Rockcliffe Hall Hotel in Huworth-on-Tees when some delicious aromas drifted from the kitchens.

"Did you smell that food?" the woman asked. "Wonderful!" Being the kind-hearted, generous man that he was, her husband thought.

"What the heck, I'll treat her!"

So they walked past a second time.

Many years ago there was a dispute between two villages, one in County Durham and the other in Northumberland. One day the villagers heard the cry, "One man from County Durham is stronger than one hundred Northumberland men."

The villagers in Northumberland were furious and immediately sent their hundred strongest men to engage with the enemy. They listened, horrified by the screams and shouts. After hours of fighting, all was quiet but none of the men returned.

Later on, the same voice shouted out, "Is that the best you can do?"

This fired up the people from Northumberland and they rallied round, getting a thousand men to do battle. After days of the most frightful blood-curdling sounds, one man emerged from the battlefield, barely able to speak, but with his last breath he managed to murmur, "It's a trap, there's two of them!"

Did you hear about the truck driver from Castle Morpeth who was seen desperately chiselling away at the brickwork after his lorry became stuck at the entrance to a tunnel?

"Why don't you let some air out of your tyres?" asked a helpful passerby.

BEWARE LOW BRIDGE!

"No, kidda," replied the driver, "It's the roof that won't go under, not the wheels."

A pupil at a school in Stockton-on-Tees said to his teacher, "Please, miss, Ah 'ave na gotta pencil."

The teacher replied, "It is: I haven't got a pencil. He hasn't got a pencil. She hasn't got a pencil. We haven't got a pencil. They haven't got a pencil."

The little boy looked puzzled then he said, "Well, miss, who has got all the blooming pencils then?"

For a minute Blyth Spartans were in with a chance – then the game started.

A man's car stalls on a country road in the Hamsterley Forest. When he gets out to fix it, a horse in the nearby field comes up alongside the fence and leans over.

"Your trouble is probably in the injectors," says the horse.

Startled, the man jumps back and runs down the road until he meets a farmer. He tells the farmer his story.

"Was it a large white horse with a black mark ower the reet eye?" asks the farmer.

"Yes, yes," the agitated man replies.

"Oh, Ah wouldn't listen to her," says the farmer, "she dinnit know owt about cars."

In the staff canteen, Jack was always showing Bob photos of his dog and saying how clever it was: doing tricks, playing ball, bringing his newspaper and slippers. One day Jack brought in the album from his daughter's wedding so Bob could look through the photos. Bob decided to tease Jack a little and said, "Hang on, where`s yewer precious dog? Ah'm surprised he wasn't the Best Man!"

Jack looked at Bob as if he was stupid, "Dinna taak se fond, someone had to take the photos."

When the manager of Morpeth Town F.C. started to tell the team about tactics, half the players thought he was talking about a new kind of peppermint.

Have you heard about the latest machine in the arcade in Durham?

You put ten pence in and ask it any question and it gives you a true answer.

One visitor from Northumberland tried it last week.
He asked the machine "Where is my father?"

The machine replied: "Your father is fishing on the River Tweed."
"Well," he thought, "That's daft for a start because my father is dead."

Next he asked, "Where is my mother's husband?"

The reply came back, "Your mother's husband is buried in Alnwick, but your father is still fishing on the River Tweed."

A man walks into the fishmongers in the Horse Market in Darlington carrying a halibut under his arm. "Do you make fishcakes?' he asks.

"Of course," says the fishmonger.

"Oh good," says the man. "It's his birthday."

COUNTY DURHAM Wit & Humour

A lad from Derwentside went for a job interview. It was going quite well until the interviewer handed him a laptop and said, "Sell this to me." So the lad put it under his arm, left the interview and went home. Half an hour later his prospective employer phoned demanding the return of the laptop. "Alreet, man," says the lad from Derwentside, "five hundred quid and it's yours."

"You're looking glum," the captain of Etherley C.C. remarked to one of his players.

"Yes, the doctor says I can't play cricket," said the downcast man. "Really?" replied the captain, "I didn't know he'd ever seen you play?"

Supporters, waiting to watch Durham City A.F.C. play Morpeth Town heard that the players driving from Northumberland were going to be delayed.

They saw a sign on the A1 that said "Clean Lavatories"... so they did.

An old chap from Shildon went to the G.P.

"Doctor," says the old boy, "Ah feel a bit cockly, you know – poorly."

"Flu?" asks the doc. "No," says the old chap, "A rode here on my bike like A always do."